1 MONTH OF
FREE
READING

at

www.ForgottenBooks.com

By purchasing this book you are eligible for one month membership to ForgottenBooks.com, giving you unlimited access to our entire collection of over 1,000,000 titles via our web site and mobile apps.

To claim your free month visit:

www.forgottenbooks.com/free111143

* Offer is valid for 45 days from date of purchase. Terms and conditions apply.

ISBN 978-1-5284-7643-0
PIBN 10111143

This book is a reproduction of an important historical work. Forgotten Books uses state-of-the-art technology to digitally reconstruct the work, preserving the original format whilst repairing imperfections present in the aged copy. In rare cases, an imperfection in the original, such as a blemish or missing page, may be replicated in our edition. We do, however, repair the vast majority of imperfections successfully; any imperfections that remain are intentionally left to preserve the state of such historical works.

Forgotten Books is a registered trademark of FB &c Ltd.
Copyright © 2018 FB &c Ltd.
FB &c Ltd, Dalton House, 60 Windsor Avenue, London, SW19 2RR.
Company number 08720141. Registered in England and Wales.

For support please visit www.forgottenbooks.com

The Finance Commission

OF THE

CITY OF BOSTON

A Chronology of the Boston Public Schools

CITY OF BOSTON
PRINTING DEPARTMENT
1912

LA306
.B7A4

NOTE.

This chronology originally was prepared for the Boston Finance Commission by George A. O. Ernst to assist in the preparation by the commission of its report upon the Boston Public Schools.

It contains a reference to all statutes, whether general or special, which affect the Boston schools; and to a variety of matters which show how the schools have developed. It goes into greater detail as to the work of the last six years than as to that of the early years because the present situation in the schools is the real purpose of the study, and the past is chiefly of value as it explains the present. Enough, however, is given to show the line of growth and the fact that there is hardly one of the great accomplishments of the present which has not proved its worth through a long persistent struggle.

Thus the unification of the school system, foreshadowed in 1830 by Chief Justice Shaw in his attempt to do away with the grotesque "double headed system"; urged by Horace Mann soon after the establishment of the State Board of Education in 1837; bitterly resisted for many years by members of the School Committee, of the Primary School Committee and of the teaching force, is now almost universally accepted, and even its critics would be unwilling to go back to the old days of decentralization.

Many subjects opposed at first as fads, frills and fancies have through their worth obtained permanent places in the school system. Drawing, "permitted" in 1827, an "ornamental branch" in 1848, "compulsory" in 1870, is the foundation stone of our industrial schools. Sewing was taught as early as 1818, but in 1876 an opinion was obtained from the City Solicitor that spending the city's money for the purpose was illegal.

It, however, met such a popular need that it was at once legalized by the Legislature. Physical training, first recognized officially in 1833, has had to fight its way to full recognition, and in some of its forms is still regarded as a "fad" or "frill."

The much discussed change from nine to eight grades in the elementary schools has sometimes been said to have been imported from a western city together with the present superintendent. As a matter of fact it had been favorably considered much earlier. In 1894 the experiment of parallel courses of seven and nine years (four and six years in the grammar schools) was tried. In 1900, two years before the present superintendent came to Boston as a supervisor, the School Committee, after a careful report and upon the favorable recommendation of the Board of Supervisors, instructed that Board to prepare a revised course of study providing for eight grades instead of nine. It was, however, not adopted until 1906.

The great wrong to teachers and pupils of excessively large classes has long been felt. In 1880 (when the standard class was 56) it was pointed out that there were sometimes 70 pupils in a class, and the duty of the School Committee to reduce the number was forcibly urged; but not until 1900 (a delay of 20 years) was the standard reduced from 56 to 50. In 1906 this vital problem was taken up seriously, and the quota of pupils to teachers has since been steadily reduced to 44, and there are plans for a further reduction.

These are typical instances of what may be found in the chronology, and show the purpose for which it was made, and the manner in which it is to be used.

A CHRONOLOGY OF THE BOSTON PUBLIC SCHOOLS.

Abbreviations: W. A.— Wightman's Annals of the Primary Schools. S. D.— School Document. S. M.— School Minutes.

1635.— Latin School, for boys only, established as the first public school in Boston. This was a year before the foundation of Harvard College and more than three years before that institution was opened. (S. D. 3 of 1905, p. 56.) It is probable that the elementary as well as the higher branches of education were taught, but its main purpose soon became the fitting of young men for college. (W. A., p. 1; S. D. 18 of 1888, p. 52; S. D. 3 of 1903, p. 9.)

1641.— The town voted that "Deare Island shall be improved for the maintanance of a Free Schoole for the Towne" and in 1649 Long and Spectacle Islands were leased, the rental to be for the use of the school. (W. A., p. 2.)

1642.— Selectmen required by law to " have a vigilant eye over their brethren and neighbors; to see that none of them shall suffer so much barbarism in any of their families as not to endeavor to teach their children and apprentices so much learning as may enable them perfectly to read the English tongue and obtain a knowledge of the capital laws." (Laws and Liberties, p. 16; S. D. 25 of 1880, p. 3.)

1647.— Every township of 50 householders required to appoint a teacher of children "to write and read," and of 100 householders to "set up a grammar schoole the master thereof being able to instruct youth so farr as they may be fitted for the university." (S. D. 25 of 1880, p. 4.)

1682.— Schools established under vote at town meeting held December 18, 1682, "for the teachinge of children to write and Cypher" under writing masters (S. D. 18 of 1888, p. 34), open to boys only; "the beginning of the common schools in Boston." (S. D. 3 of 1903, p. 14.)

1683.— Every town of 500 families or householders required to "set up and maintain two grammar schools and two writing schools." (Colonial Laws, p. 305.)

1692.— Province Laws require towns of 50 householders to provide "a schoolmaster to teach children and youth to read and write," and of 100 householders a grammar school to be conducted by a "discreet person of good conversation well instructed in the tongues." (Prov. Laws, 1692-93, Chap. 26.)

1701.— Grammar masters to be approved by ministers by certificate under their hands. (Prov. Laws 1701-2, Chap. 10.)

1740.— Grammar masters as distinguished from writing masters appointed in Boston to teach reading, grammar, geography and other higher studies, beginning the "double-headed system" of divided authority between writing masters and grammar masters. The children in each school were divided into two parts, the one attending in the forenoon in the grammar master's room, which was usually upstairs, and in the afternoon in the writing master's room, which was usually downstairs; while the other part attended in the reverse order. (S. D. 3 of 1903, p. 15.)

1751.— A committee reported to the town that "the charge of supporting the several Publick Schools amounted the last year to more than one-third part of the whole sum drawn for by the selectmen." (S. D. 18 of 1888, p. 37.)

1762.— The town voted that the treasurer be directed to borrow 1,500 pounds for the payment of the schoolmasters' salaries then due (S. D. 18 of 1888, p. 38), an early instance of the payment of current expenses from loans.

1789.— Every town or district of 50, 100 or 150 householders required to provide schoolmasters of good morals for varying school terms "to teach children to read & write & to instruct them in the english language as well as in arithmetic, orthography and decent behavior," and of 200 families or householders to provide "a grammar schoolmaster of good morals well instructed in the latin, greek and english languages," no youth to be sent to such schools, without permission from the Selectmen, "unless they shall have learned in some other school or in some other way to read the english language by spelling the same." (Acts of 1789, Chap. 19.)

School Committee chosen, consisting of Selectmen and one member from each ward. (W. A., p. 7; S. D. 18 of 1888, p. 7.)

Girls first admitted to the Boston public schools, but only from 20th April to 20th October in each year. "This was doubtless because many of the boys had work to do in the summer season, and so left room in the schools for the girls." (S. D. 3 of 1903, p. 14.) There was a thorough reorganization of the school system; the age limit of admission to the reading and writing schools was fixed at seven, pupils to be allowed to continue until the age of fourteen. (S. D. 18 of 1888, p 39.)

1793.— Franklin medals to boys only first awarded, though dated 1792. (W. A., p. 8.)

1812.— Appropriation "towards maintaining a school for African children." Prior to this time, colored children who so desired attended white schools. (City Doc. 23 of 1846, p. 15.)

1816.— Sunday schools (private) first established in Boston, the object being to teach children to read and write as well as to give religious instruction. This brought out the fact that a large proportion of children could neither read nor write, and to them therefore under the law of 1789, quoted above, the doors of the public schools were shut. This was one of the causes which led to the establishment of primary schools. (W. A., p. 12; S. D. 18 of 1888, p. 13.)

1818.— Primary schools first established in Boston although opposed by the Selectmen and School Committee (W. A., p. 35), for children between four and seven years of age under a Primary School Committee of 36 members appointed by, but with authority independent of, the regular School Committee (W. A., p. 72); the origin of the distinction long recognized between primary and grammar schools (S. D. 3 of 1902, p. 45) which was not until 1906 wholly abandoned. (S. D. 9 of 1906, p. 28.) In these schools the girls were taught knitting or sewing. (W. A., p. 44.)

1820.— First "intermediate school" established for illiterate children over seven years of age, who were too old to be admitted to the primary schools, and under the law of 1789, because of their illiteracy, could not be admitted to the grammar schools. Investigation showed that there were a large number of such children. (W. A., p. 53.)

1821.— English Classical (now High) School established for boys who were to be prepared not for the university but for various mercantile and mechanical pursuits. In later years it has become important as a fitting school for the higher institutions, like the Massachusetts Institute of Technology and Harvard College. (S. D. 3 of 1903, pp. 39, 42.)

City medals for girls instituted as an offset to the Franklin medals for boys; abolished in 1847; restored in 1848; but finally given up, and diplomas substituted. (S. D. 18 of 1888, p. 42.)

1822.— Under the city charter a school committee established consisting of the Mayor, aldermen and one member elected from each ward, 25 members in all. (Acts of 1821, Chap. 110.)

1826.— High School for Girls established, but the number of girls applying was so great that it was given up in 1828; in other words, it was too successful. (S. D. 18 of 1888, p. 47; S. D. 3 of 1903, p. 43.)

Text-books required by law to be furnished to pupils "at such prices as merely to reimburse to the town the expense of procuring the same"; free to those unable to pay. Teachers must obtain from School Committee a certificate of fitness to instruct. (Acts of 1825–26, Chap. 170.)

1827.— In addition to studies previously required, towns of 500 families required to provide a master competent to teach history of the United States, book-keeping by single entry, geometry, surveying and algebra, and where there were 4,000 inhabitants general history, rhetoric and logic. No books to be used or purchased "calculated to favor any particular religious sect or tenet." Provision as to teachers' certificate of qualifications. (Acts of 1826–27, Chap. 143.)

1827.— Drawing introduced as a "permitted" subject in the English High School. (S. D. 3 of 1903, p. 97.)

1828.— High School for Girls discontinued, but girls admitted to grammar and writing schools throughout the year. (S. D. 18 of 1888, p. 48.)

1830.— "Infant Schools," forerunners of the kindergarten, having been established by private societies and individuals, were considered adversely by the Primary School Committee. (W. A., p. 123; S. D. 3 of 1903, p. 30.)

Chief Justice Shaw, then a member of the School Committee, attacked the "double-headed system" and urged the "single-headed system" (the supremacy of the grammar masters), but without immediate effect, the change (although tried in 1836 in two schools) not being permanently adopted until 1847. "With all the sound arguments of reason and experience on its side, a campaign of no less than seventeen years was necessary to bring its merit into general recognition. Like many another school reform it was seen to be inimical to what the schoolmasters (*i. e.*, the writing masters) were pleased to regard as their vested rights and interests." (S. D. 3 of 1903, p. 16.)

Chief Justice Shaw also advocated, but more successfully, the education of the sexes in separate school buildings. This is the origin of separate schools in the older parts of Boston. (S. D. 3 of 1903, p. 18.)

Attempt to introduce music as a regular study in the public schools. (S. D. 15 of 1888, p. 3.)

1833.— Interesting exhibition of conservatism in resisting introduction into the primary schools of books, maps, globes, or anything outside the established curriculum, the Board refusing not on sanitary grounds but from pure conservatism a request of a member to introduce experimentally at his own expense a blackboard, slates and pencils. (W. A., p. 136 *et seq.*) Public sentiment was strongly in favor of the innovations and the Board later provided slates and pencils. (W. A., p. 149.) Blackboards were also subsequently provided, and there was a gradual increase in educational helps. (S. D. 3 of 1903, p. 30.)

First official action as to physical education in primary schools. (S D. 22 of 1891, p. 26; W. A., p. 149.)

Children over eight years of age admitted into the grammar schools, although not qualified by their attainments, provided their parents or guardians obtained permission of the sub-committee in charge. (W. A., p. 148.)

1834.— Act reorganizing School Committee to consist of Mayor and twenty members elected at large, ten each year for two years (Acts of 1834, Chap. 158), not accepted by the people.

1835.— School Committee reorganized, to consist of Mayor, president of Common Council, and two members elected from each ward, 26 members in all. (Acts of 1835, Chap. 128.)

1835.— Sewing, which had been taught in primary schools, authorized in writing schools. (S. D. 24 of 1881, p. 3; S. D. 18 of 1888, p. 72.)

1836.— Drawing made "obligatory" in the English High School, but no teacher of drawing appointed until 1853. (S. D. 3 of 1903, p. 97.)

1837.— State Board of Education established (Acts of 1837, Chap. 241), and Horace Mann elected Secretary. (S. D. 18 of 1888, p. 26.)

1838.— Beginning of the controversies (W. A., p. 175) which ended with the abolition of the Primary School Committee in 1855. (W. A., p. 259.) The Primary Board in principle and practice was in direct antagonism (id., p. 277) to the doctrine of centralization advocated by Horace Mann, who urged making the educational system a "unit" and placing it under the supervision of a Superintendent of Public Schools (id., p. 266). The primary system was an extreme illustration of decentralization, each primary teacher with her school being an independent entity. (S. D. 3 of 1902, p. 45.)

School Committees to make annual reports; and to select and make contracts with teachers. (Acts of 1838, Chap. 105.)

City Council passed order authorizing the Primary School Committee to admit children over seven who were not qualified for admission to the grammar schools; development of "Intermediate Schools." (W. A., p. 173; see also id., p. 55.)

Music (singing) introduced into schools. (S. D. 15 of 1888, p. 4; S. D. 3 of 1903, p. 89.)

1841.— Brighton High School established. (S. D. 18 of 1888, p. 50.)

1844.— School Committee authorized to dismiss any teacher from the service, compensation thereupon immediately to cease. (Acts of 1844, Chap. 32.)

Bitter attack upon Horace Mann and his famous "Seventh Report" by "31 Boston Grammar Masters." (Martin's Evolution of the Massachusetts Public School System, p. 181. For titles of pamphlets in the controversy which followed see Barnard's Journal of Education, Vol. 5, p. 651.)

1845.— Severe comment by Committee on Examinations upon examination papers written by grammar pupils of this year. (City Doc. 26 of 1845.)

Colored citizens petition for the abolition of special schools for colored children — majority and minority reports thereon. (City Doc. 23 of 1846.) Primary School Committee voted against the change. (W. A., pp. 209, 214.)

Primary School Committee voted, 46 to 18, against establishing position of Superintendent. (W. A., p. 211.)

1847.— Appropriation of money authorized for schools to teach "adults reading, writing, English grammar, arithmetic and geography." (Acts of 1847, Chap. 137.)

1847.— John D. Philbrick appointed master of the Quincy School, a substantial victory of the "single-headed system," which in a few years thereafter became universal in Boston, the writing master gradually disappearing, authority being given to the grammar master, an important step towards unification. As an illustration of the difficulty of dispensing with superfluous employees it may be noted that one of the writing masters drew pay until his death in 1877, at the age of 96, although for many years he rendered no service, but was annually appointed as an "assistant teacher." (S. D. 3 of 1903, p. 17; S. M. of 1876, p. 200.)

Report of committee in favor of free text-books to all pupils. (Doc. 38 of 1847.)

1848.— Drawing placed on the list of grammar school studies, but treated as an "ornamental branch," and little done with it until 1871. (S. D. 3 of 1903, p. 97.)

Charlestown High School established. (S. D. 18 of 1888, p. 50.)

1849.— Eliot (now West Roxbury) High School established. (S. D. 18 of 1888, p. 50.)

1850.— Public schools to be supplied with dictionaries at state expense. (Resolves of 1850, Chap. 99.)

Physiology and hygiene authorized to be taught in the public schools and all teachers required to be examined thereon. (Acts of 1850, Chap. 229.)

First truant law enacted in Massachusetts for children between six and fifteen years of age. (Acts of 1850, Chap. 294.) (For subsequent truant legislation see S. D. 25 of 1880.)

1851.— Office of Superintendent established; Nathan Bishop elected as first Superintendent of the Boston Public Schools; held office until 1856. (S. D. 3 of 1903, p. 58; W. A., p. 266 et seq.)

1852.— Compulsory school age to be "between the ages of eight and fourteen years." (Acts of 1852, Chap. 240.)

Normal School established for the purpose of preparing young women to become teachers. (S. D. 4 of 1895, p. 297.)

Roxbury High School and Dorchester High School established. (S. D. 18 of 1888, pp. 48 and 50.)

1853.— Rule established that "every scholar shall have daily in the forenoon and afternoon some kind of physical or gymnastic exercise." (S. D. 22 of 1891, p. 27.)

1854.— School Committee reorganized to consist of Mayor, president of Common Council, and six elected from each ward, in all 74 members. (Acts of 1854, Chap. 448, Sect. 53.)

General law authorizing cities and towns to establish position of Superintendent of Schools. (Acts of 1854, Chap. 314.) Boston had already appointed a Superintendent in 1851.

High School courses for girls introduced in the Normal School and name changed to the Girls' High and Normal School. (S. D. 4 of 1895, p. 297.)

1854.— High School for Girls established in Roxbury. (S. D. 18 of 1888, p. 49.)

Sewing, heretofore "authorized," now required to be taught in 4th class of the Grammar Schools for Girls. (S. D. 24 of 1881, p. 4.)

1855.— Primary School Committee (established in 1818), which had grown to 196 members, abolished (by the charter amendments of 1854) and jurisdiction over the primary schools transferred to regular School Committee, but the distinction between primary and grammar schools and the independence of primary schools, through primary sub-committees, continued. (W. A., p. 264; S. D. 18 of 1888, p. 29; S. D. 3 of 1903, p. 34 *et seq.*)

Cities and towns authorized to furnish school books and stationery at their own expense. (Acts of 1855, Chap. 436 — repealed in 1857; Acts of 1857, Chap. 206.)

Daily reading of some portion of the Bible in the common English version required. (Acts of 1855, Chap. 410.)

Distinction on account of race, color or religion in admission to public schools forbidden. (Acts of 1855, Chap. 256.)

Amendment to the Constitution forbidding school moneys to be appropriated for sectarian schools. (Article XVIII.)

Compulsory vaccination law. (Acts of 1855, Chap. 414.)

1856.— John D. Philbrick elected Superintendent; continued in office except for a brief interval until 1878. (S. D. 3 of 1903, p. 19.)

1857.— Schools for persons over fifteen years of age authorized, to be held either in the day or evening, the School Committee to determine subjects to be taught. (Acts of 1857, Chap. 189.)

Teachers must be competent to teach (in addition to previously required studies) algebra and the history of the United States in towns of 50 or more families; natural philosophy, chemistry, botany, and civil polity of the Commonwealth and the United States, in towns of 500 families; and French, astronomy, geology, intellectual and moral science, and political economy in towns of 4,000 inhabitants. (Acts of 1857, Chap. 206.)

Children between the ages of five and fifteen years entitled to attend school where they reside, but nonresident parent or guardian must pay for the tuition a sum equal to the average expense per scholar for such school. (Acts of 1857, Chap. 132.)

Superintendent Philbrick recommended classification in primary schools, and that each pupil be supplied with a single desk and chair, and also with a slate; adopted and carried into effect. Prior to this, each primary teacher had charge of six classes, and carried the pupils under her care through the whole preparation for the grammar school. (S. D. 18 of 1888, p. 30.)

1858.— Standing Committee on Music established, and special instructors appointed. (For history of music in the schools see School Committee Report of 1858, p. 45; S. D. 3 of 1903, p. 89.)

1859.— School books to be furnished to scholars at net cost; when a change is made the School Committee shall furnish the substituted book to each pupil requiring it at the expense of the city or town. (Acts of 1859, Chap. 93.)

School Committees to select and contract with teachers; require satisfactory evidence of the good moral character of all instructors, and ascertain by personal examination their qualifications for teaching and capacity for the government of schools. (Acts of 1859, Chap. 60; see Rev. St., Chap. 23, Sect. 13; Acts of 1838, Chap. 105.)

1860.— Special committee appointed to consider the subject of physical training. (S. D. 7 of 1890, p. 24.)

1861.— Minimum age of admission to primary schools raised from four to five years. (S. D. 18 of 1888, p. 31.)

Roxbury High Schools for boys and girls united into single school. (S. D. 18 of 1888, p. 49.)

1862.— Agriculture authorized to be taught by lectures or otherwise in the public schools. (Acts of 1862, Chap. 7.)

Bible to be read daily without note or comment; no scholar to be required to read from any particular version whose parent or guardian declares he has conscientious scruples against it; no school book to be purchased or used calculated to favor the tenets of any particular sect of Christians. (Acts of 1862, Chap. 57.)

1863.— State Board of Education directed by Legislature to report concerning the introduction in schools of military drill. (Resolves of 1863, Chap. 66.)

1864.— Military drill introduced, although the Legislature refused to pass bills authorizing it. (S. D. 22 of 1891, p. 41.)

Instruction in physical culture introduced under orders passed by the School Committee which have been called the "great charter of Physical Training in the Boston schools." (S. D. 18 of 1888, p. 76; S. D. 22 of 1891, p. 43.) The latter document contains an elaborate study of physical training and of its history in Boston.

1866.— Masters of grammar schools given duties of principal, both in the grammar and primary schools of their respective districts. This attempt at unification met with opposition from some of the masters who were "incompetent or unwilling to exercise a helpful control over the methods of primary teaching"; and from many of the teachers who "were slow to co-operate either with the master or with each other." It continued until 1879, when jurisdiction over primary schools was temporarily taken away from the grammar masters but restored in 1882. (S. D. 18 of 1888, p. 31; see also S. D. 3 of 1902, p. 45.)

1867.— Schools for licensed minors established. (S. D. 19 of 1885, p. 22.)

Corporal punishment considered. (Annual Report of 1868, p. 197; see also S. M. of 1902, p. 501; S. D. 14 of 1903, p. 6.)

1868.— First regular appropriation in Boston for evening schools, under authority of Acts of 1857, Chap. 189, a delay of eleven years. (S. D. 3 of 1903, p. 72.)

1868.— Roxbury annexed and schools taken over, including Roxbury High School. (S. D. 3 of 1903, p. 50.)

Diplomas first awarded to graduates. (S. D. 18 of 1888, p. 43.)

1869.— Evening High School first opened. (S. D. 3 of 1903, p. 73.)

Horace Mann School for the Deaf first opened. (S. D. 3 of 1903, p. 66.)

1870.— Teaching drawing in public schools and free instruction in industrial or mechanical drawing to persons over fifteen years of age in day or evening schools made compulsory in towns or cities having more than 10,000 inhabitants. (Acts of 1870, Chap. 248.)

Free Evening Industrial Drawing School first opened. (S. D. 3 of 1903, p. 75; S. D. 3 of 1905.)

Dorchester annexed and schools taken over, including Dorchester High School. (S. D. 3 of 1903, p. 50.)

First kindergarten established, believed to be the first public free kindergarten in the world. (S. D. 2 of 1888, p. 18.)

Change from four grammar grades to six, making with three primary grades nine grades below the high schools; beginning of the nine-grade system in Boston. (S. D. 3 of 1904, p. 49.)

1871.— Drawing first taken seriously in the schools through the movement for industrial art education. (S. D. 3 of 1903, p. 97.)

1872.— Industrial schools authorized; the School Committee to "prescribe the arts, trades and occupations to be taught," and to have the management thereof. (Acts of 1872, Chap. 86.)

Normal School and Girls' High School separated and each established as an independent institution. '(S. D. 18 of 1888, p. 48.)

1873. Truant officers first placed under authority of School Committee. (Acts of 1873, Chap. 262.)

Age of compulsory attendance decreased from fourteen to twelve years, but term of schooling lengthened. (Acts of 1873, Chap. 279.)

School books may be loaned to pupils. (Acts of 1873, Chap. 106.)

1874.— Age limit restored from twelve to fourteen years for compulsory attendance at school. (Acts of 1874, Chap. 233.)

Charlestown, Brighton and West Roxbury annexed and schools taken over, including high schools. (S. D. 3 of 1903, p. 50.)

The legality of using the city's money for the Normal School having been questioned (S. D. 3 of 1903, p. 59), its establishment was legalized by the Legislature. (Acts of 1874, Chap. 167.)

1875.— School Committee, having by annexation and the city's growth increased to 116 members, was reorganized and the number reduced to 25 (beginning January, 1876), to consist of the Mayor and 24 members elected at large in groups of 8 each, serving three years. (Acts of 1875, Chap. 241; S. D. 18 of 1888, p. 8.)

Power given School Committee to appoint janitors. (Acts of 1875, Chap. 241.)

Power given School Committee to decide as to necessity and location of school buildings and alterations costing over $1,000, but appropriations to be made by and work done through City Council. (Acts of 1875, Chap. 241.)

1875.— School Committee to elect a Superintendent and Board of not exceeding six Supervisors for terms of two years, a Secretary and Auditing Clerk. (Acts of 1875, Chap. 241.)

1876.— Under the new School Committee, the rules and regulations were revised, and a large apparent power was given to the Superintendent and Supervisors, but real power was retained in sub-committees. (Rules and Regulations of 1876; S. D. 18 of 1888, p. 30; S. D. 4 of 1896, p. 85.)

The fitness of candidates for the teaching force was, under the rules, to be determined by examinations to be held by the Supervisors by whom "Certificates of Qualification" were to be granted. (Rules and Regulations of 1876; S. D. 5 of 1889, p. 25.)

Law as to change of text-books amended to require a two-thirds vote of the entire committee. (Acts of 1876, Chap. 47.)

City Solicitor having ruled that the city's money could not legally be spent in the teaching of sewing (S. D. 18 of 1888, p. 73) (although it had been taught for many years), it was legalized by the Legislature. (Acts of 1876, Chap. 3.)

Establishing office of Medical Inspector of Schools considered, but City Solicitor advised that the committee had no legal right to spend money for the purpose. (S. M. of 1876, p. 214; S. M. of 1877, p. 51; S. D. 20 of 1889, p. 5.)

1877.— School Committee incorporated with authority to hold property in trust. (Acts of 1877, Chap. 53.)

A truant officer with the title of Superintendent of Licensed Minors assigned to schools for licensed minors. (S. D. 19 of 1885, p. 22.)

1878.— Samuel Eliot elected Superintendent. (S. M. of 1878, p. 12.) Remained in office until 1880.

East Boston High School established. (S. D. 3 of 1903, p. 52.)

Girls' Latin School established for the express purpose of fitting girls for college. (S. D. 3 of 1903, p. 53.)

Stationery may be supplied free. (Acts of 1878, Chap. 23.)

Nautical schools authorized by law. (Acts of 1878, Chap. 159.)

1879.— Supervision of primary schools taken from grammar masters and placed in charge of Supervisors. (S. D. 10 of 1879; S. D. 4 of 1880, pp. 3, 62; S. D. 18 of 1888, p. 31.)

Elaborate reports on proposed revision of the school system. (S. D. 4 to 12 of 1879.)

Report on Industrial Education, with especial reference to the establishment of a Free Industrial Institute for the education of mechanics, consisting of a developing school and school shops, recommending its establishment. (S. D. 25 of 1879.)

Kindergarten and intermediate schools discontinued. (S. D. 30 of 1879, p. 9.)

Pensions for teachers suggested tentatively. (S. D. 30 of 1879, p. 37; see also S. D. 5 of 1880, p. 6; S. D. 10 of 1880.)

Women authorized to vote for School Committee. (Acts of 1879, Chap. 223.)

1880.— Law amended so that no pupil shall be required to take any personal part in reading the Bible whose parent or guardian informs the teacher that he has conscientious scruples against it. (Acts of 1880, Chap. 176.)

1880.— Committee on primary school instruction reported as to excessive number of children in various classes, sometimes as high as seventy, and said "forty children are all that one woman can attend to properly," adding that it is "the first duty of the Board to remedy this great wrong." (S. D. 1 of 1880, p. 5.) At this time fifty-six pupils to a teacher was the standard, with thirty-five in ungraded classes. (Rules and Regulations for 1879, section 216.)

City Solicitor having ruled (S. M. of 1880, p. 122) that an Instructor in Hygiene might be appointed, but that he could not have duties of medical inspector, a controversy in the committee arose and not until 1885 was the position filled. (S. D. 20 of 1889.)

Report of Committee on Truant Officers giving an historical sketch of this branch of the school system. (S. D. 25 of 1880.)

Edwin P. Seaver elected Superintendent; remained in office for twenty-four years, until 1904. (S. D. 27 of 1880, p. 12; S. M. of 1880, p. 201; S. M. of 1904, p. 302.) In his first annual report he urged "a unity of purpose and a unity of method which come only from proper supervision" and "efficient co-operation." (S. D. 5 of 1881, p. 13.)

1881.— Calisthenics, gymnastics and military drill authorized by statute, and prior action of school committees in causing them to be taught ratified and confirmed. This legalized what had long been done in Boston. (Acts of 1881, Chap. 193.)

Movement to abolish suburban high schools; majority and minority reports thereon; failed because of public protest. (S. D. 8 of 1881; S. D. 26 of 1881, p. 11; S. M. of 1881, p. 132.)

A system of supplementary reading introduced. (S. D. 7 of 1881; S. D. 4 of 1882, p. 51; S. D. 3 of 1902, p. 36.)

Experiment in industrial instruction through a "carpenter's class" in the Dwight School. (S. D. 15 of 1882; S. D. 4 of 1883, p. 39.)

Historical account of sewing in the schools. (S. D. 24 of 1881, p. 8.)

1882.— Supervision of primary schools taken from the Supervisors and restored to grammar masters, the value of unification being now more fully recognized. (S. D. 2 of 1882; S. D. 4 of 1882, p. 18; S. D. 21 of 1882, p. 17; S. D. 3 of 1903, p. 37.)

The City Solicitor having ruled that the city could not legally provide instruction in the Normal School for the benefit of teachers in the service of the city (S. D. 4 of 1882, p. 46), the Legislature gave authority. (Acts of 1882, Chap. 136.)

1883.— Evening schools compulsory in towns and cities of 10,000 or more inhabitants "for the instruction of persons over 12 years of age in orthography, reading, writing, geography, arithmetic, drawing, history of the United States, and good behavior," and such other subjects as the School Committee shall deem expedient. (Acts of 1883, Chap. 174.)

1883.— Importance of industrial education discussed by Superintendent Seaver, outlining a central school which later was realized in the Mechanic Arts High School. A Committee on Industrial Education reported in favor of manual training as a part of the course of instruction in the public schools. At this early day the modern distinction between manual training and industrial education does not appear to have been accepted. (S. D. 4 of 1883, p. 34; S. D. 19 of 1883; S. D. 15 of 1889; S. D. 18 of 1897, p. 33; S. D. 4 of 1901, p. 34.)

1884.— Text-books and other school supplies required to be furnished free to all pupils. (Acts of 1884, Chap. 103; S. D. 19 of 1884, p. 12.)

Manual training first introduced, under provisions of Acts of 1884, Chap. 69, authorizing instruction in the "elementary use of hand tools" which were to be bought and loaned free to pupils. Rooms in the basement of the Latin School building were fitted with tools and benches, and a class of 200 boys from the grammar schools was taught carpentry and cabinet making. (S. D. 19 of 1884, p. 18.)

Pupils forbidden to attend public schools while or within two weeks after any member of the household is sick of small-pox, diphtheria, or scarlet fever. (Acts of 1884, Chap. 64; see also Acts of 1885, Chap. 198.)

Permanent corps of substitute teachers suggested. (S. D. 4 of 1884, p. 12; see also S. D. 4 of 1895, p. 84.)

Movement to reduce number of Supervisors from six to four unsuccessful. (S. D. 3 of 1884; S. M. of 1884, p. 53.)

Rules amended to increase the executive powers of the Superintendent. (S. M. of 1884, p. 171.)

1885.— Mayor no longer a member of the School Committee, but he is given a qualified veto on orders, resolutions or votes of the School Committee involving the expenditure of money. (Acts of 1885, Chap. 266, Sect. 10.)

Teaching of physiology and hygiene, including effect of alcoholic drinks, etc., made compulsory in the public schools. (Acts of 1885, Chap. 332.)

Office of Instructor in Hygiene established. (S. M. of 1885, pp. 116, 146; S. D. 8 of 1886; S. D. 20 of 1889.)

State granted land on Newbury street to city for Horace Mann School for the Deaf. (Acts of 1885, Chap. 201.) New building erected thereon and opened in 1890. (S. D. 3 of 1903, p. 67.)

School Committee authorized to provide at expense of the city apparatus, books of reference and other means of illustration. (Acts of 1885, Chap. 161.)

The City Solicitor having ruled that attendance could not be required outside the regular schools, permission was granted to children from the Eliot and Hancock schools, whose parents or guardians so request, to attend on probation the North End Industrial Home two hours a week for manual training (S. D. 3 of 1885; S. M. of 1885, p. 90), and girls from Winthrop,

Franklin, Everett, Hyde and Wells schools authorized to attend the Tennyson street school of cookery. (S. D. 19 of 1885, p. 28.)

1885.— Schools for licensed minors discontinued, and position of Superintendent of Licensed Minors abolished, pupils being transferred to ungraded classes. (S. D. 19 of 1885, p. 23.)

1886.— First schools of cookery opened at city's expense. (S. M. of 1886, pp. 124, 184; S. D. 4 of 1895, p. 281; S. D. 3 of 1903, p. 107.)

Parental School for truants authorized (Acts of 1886, Chap. 282), but in spite of repeated requests from School Committee not established by City Council until 1895 (S. D. 23 of 1890, p. 38; S. D. 20 of 1891; S. D. 3 of 1903, p. 85), truants in the meanwhile being sent to Deer Island. (S. D. 4 of 1885, p. 67.)

Election of teachers on tenure authorized. (Acts of 1886, Chap. 313.) Adopted in Boston in 1889. (S. M. of 1889, pp. 67, 77.)

Evening high school required by law to be established in cities of 50,000 inhabitants if requested by 50 qualified residents. (Acts of 1886, Chap. 236.)

1887.— Interesting account of the history of vacations, holidays, etc., in the schools of Boston. (S. D. 17 of 1887, p. 27.)

1888.— Kindergartens for children $3\frac{1}{2}$ years old again taken into the school system. (S. D. 18 of 1888, p. 10.)

Course in Normal School extended to $1\frac{1}{2}$ years. (S. M. of 1888, p. 245.)

Suggested reduction of pupils, from 56 to 40, in first class of grammar schools defeated. (S. M. of 1888, p. 192.)

1889.— Compulsory attendance law amended so that poverty is no longer an excuse for absence from school, and all exceptions repealed other than that the child shall have attended for the required period a private day school approved by the School Committee, or has been otherwise instructed, or has already acquired the required learning, or if his physical or mental condition renders attendance inexpedient or impracticable. (Acts of 1889, Chap. 464.)

Truant officers authorized to apprehend without a warrant and take to school any truant. (Acts of 1889, Chap. 422.)

Power of School Committee over location, erection and repairs of school buildings enlarged, but appropriations still left with City Council. (Acts of 1889, Chap. 297.)

Janitors, engineers and all persons having charge of steam boilers and furnaces in the school buildings placed under the Civil Service law. (Acts of 1889, Chap. 352.)

Establishment of a Mechanic Arts High School advocated and plan formulated by Superintendent Seaver. (S. D. 5 of 1889, p. 19.)

Boston Teachers' Mutual Benefit Association organized. (S. D. 4 of 1895, p. 73.)

Majority and minority reports on Instruction in Hygiene. (S. D. 20 of 1889.) Report of the Board of Supervisors on Physical Training. (S. D. 10 of 1889.)

1890.— School Committee authorized to erect and furnish new school buildings from loans not to exceed $550,000. (Acts of 1890, Chap. 355.)

Last regular session prior to Memorial Day to be devoted to exercises of a patriotic nature. (Acts of 1890, Chap. 111.)

Horace Mann School for Deaf transferred to new building on Newbury street. (S. D. 24 of 1890.)

Attempt to reduce quota of pupils to 49 in grammar and primary schools defeated. (S. M. of 1890, p. 105.)

Office of Instructor in Hygiene abolished and Director of Physical Training established. (S. M. of 1890, pp. 45, 210.)

Interesting majority and minority reports on coeducation of the sexes. (S. D. 19 of 1890.)

Plan of having no recess, and dismissing the morning session at 20 minutes before twelve tried in various schools (S. D. 7 of 1890, p. 27), but later given up (S. D. 12 of 1891, p. 22).

Leave of absence of one year on half pay authorized for teachers after every ninth year of service. (S. M. of 1890, pp. 227, 233.) Discontinued in 1895. (S. M. of 1895, pp. 250, 315.)

1891.— Compulsory age limit increased to 15 in cities or towns where opportunity is furnished for gratuitous instruction in the use of tools or in manual training, or for industrial education in any form. (Acts of 1891, Chap. 361.)

School Committee assented to appointment by Board of Health of medical inspectors for schools. (S. D. 19 of 1891, p. 27; S. M. of 1891, p. 301.)

Elaborate report on Physical Training. (S. D. 22 of 1891; see also S. D. 8 of 1894.)

Opinion of Corporation Counsel that the Normal School was for girls only and that men could not be admitted. (S. D. 19 of 1891, p. 10.)

1892.— Investigation and elaborate report as to proper seating of pupils and as to the injurious effect of unsuitable school furniture. (S. D. 9 of 1892; see also S. D. 8 of 1894, p. 108; S. D. 4 of 1895, p. 169.)

Course in Normal School extended to two years. (S. M. of 1892, p. 189.)

1893.— Truant officers placed under Civil Service law. (Acts of 1893, Chap. 253.)

Mechanic Arts High School established. (S. D. 3 of 1903, p. 54.)

Cities and towns maintaining free evening schools authorized to provide lectures on natural sciences, history and kindred subjects. (Acts of 1893, Chap. 208.)

Omission of, and substitute plan for, diploma examinations, and for promotions from primary to grammar schools. (S. M. of 1893, pp. 291, 331; S. D. 15 of 1895, p. 13; S. M. of 1895, p. 353.)

1894.— Manual Training in high schools made compulsory by law after September 1, 1895, in cities of 20,000 or more inhabitants, the course of instruction to "be subject to the approval of the State Board of Education." (Acts of 1894, Chap. 471.)

1894.— Instruction in cooking authorized (although Boston had schools of cookery since 1886), and the requirement as to instruction "in the elementary use of hand tools" changed to "the use of tools." Tools, implements and materials required to be loaned to pupils free of charge. (Acts of 1894, Chap. 320.)

Vivisection in public schools prohibited in the presence of any scholar, child or minor. (Acts of 1894, Chap. 151.)

Compulsory school law amended in certain details. (Acts of 1894, Chap. 188.) Law as to compulsory attendance and truancy codified. (Acts of 1894, Chap. 498.)

Medical Visitors (Inspectors) for the schools established by the Board of Health. (S. D. 4 of 1895, p. 76; S. D. 4 of 1900, p. 38.)

Special committee appointed to consider giving the Superintendent and Board of Supervisors greater power and responsibility reported in favor thereof (S. D. 7 of 1894), and their recommendations were adopted; but real power continued in sub-committees. (S. M. of 1894, pp. 199 to 207; S. D. 19 of 1894, p. 10; S. D. 4 of 1896, p. 86.)

Report on secondary education by Committee of Ten of the National Educational Association (of which President Eliot was chairman) considered by Superintendent Seaver, in the course of which he discussed the regrading of classes "in such a way as to give eight years or grades below the high school." (S. D. 4 of 1894, pp. 5, 12, 28 and 29; see also S. D. 19 of 1894, p. 18; S. D. 4 of 1896, p. 46.)

Departmental instruction in grammar schools authorized. (S. D. 20 of 1893; S. M. of 1894, p. 47; S. D. 19 of 1894, p. 15; S. D. 5 of 1897, p. 47; S. D. 4 of 1900, p. 17.)

Experiment authorized of parallel courses of study of four and six years in grammar schools. (S. D. 19 of 1894, p. 16; S. D. 4 of 1895, p. 27.)

1895.— Foreign flags forbidden on outside of schools (Acts of 1895, Chap. 115) and United States flag required to be provided for each schoolhouse. (Acts of 1895, Chap. 181.)

School Committee given full power to erect and furnish school buildings; Street Commissioners to take land at request of School Committee; bonds authorized. (Acts of 1895, Chap. 408.)

Latin, French, algebra and geometry, and other "enrichment studies" introduced in certain grammar schools experimentally. (S. D. 4 of 1895, p. 37; S. D. 4 of 1896, p. 41; S. D. 5 of 1897, p. 42.)

Position of Director of Kindergartens established. (S. M. of 1894, p. 348.)

Parental School for truants established in West Roxbury (under Acts of 1886, Chap. 282) after many efforts by the School Committee to secure action by City Council, under jurisdiction of directors of public institutions (now Children's Institutions Department), subject to visitation by School Committee. (S. D. 3 of 1903, p. 85.)

1896.— Supervision of drawing in day schools restored, and a staff of assistants to the Director appointed. (S. D. 3 of 1903, p. 100.)

Transfer of Normal School to State considered, and defeated. (S. M. of 1896, p. 523; S. D. 5 of 1897, p. 16.)

1897.— Additional loans authorized, of which not less than $500,000 to be used for new high school buildings in East Boston, South Boston, West Roxbury and Dorchester. (Acts of 1897, Chap. 442.)

Board of Supervisors report in favor of a Girls' High School of Practical Arts. (S. D. 10 of 1897.)

Commercial courses in high schools authorized but not introduced until 1898. (S. D. 19 of 1897, p. 30; S. D. 15 of 1898, p. 18.)

Rules amended giving to the Board of Supervisors (instead of to the sub-committees) the initiative in the appointment of teachers. (S. D. 19 of 1897, p. 26 et seq.)

1898.— School Committee given power (formerly in City Council) to make appropriations from tax rate within prescribed limits for the support of the public schools, including repairs and alterations upon school buildings. (Acts of 1898, Chap. 400.)

Important changes in rules giving Superintendent and Supervisors greater power, and reducing the powers of sub-committees; the appointment, transfer and removal of teachers being given to the Superintendent, subject to the approval of the School Committee. Attempt made but failed to abolish sub-committees. (S. D. 15 of 1898, p. 13; S. D. 11 of 1898.)

Merit list established for the appointment of teachers from graduates of Normal School (S. D. 3 of 1899, p. 13), thus for the first time introducing the Civil Service idea in the appointment of teachers. (S. D. 4 of 1900, p. 13.)

School Committee voted in May to discontinue the Normal School in the hope that the State would take it over, but the popular protest was so great that in November the vote was rescinded. (S. M. of 1898, pp. 310, 574; S. D. 3 of 1903, p. 60.)

Additional loans for high and Latin schools authorized. (Acts of 1898, Chap. 149.)

Law as to school attendance and truancy amended and codified. Compulsory age limit "between seven and fourteen." A child need not be vaccinated upon certificate of a practicing physician that such child is an unfit subject therefor. Measles added to list of contagious diseases. (Acts of 1898, Chap. 496.)

Manual Training made compulsory in both elementary and high schools. (Acts of 1898, Chap. 496, Sect. 4.)

Evening schools required to teach the English language and grammar, industrial drawing, both freehand and mechanical, physiology and hygiene, in addition to previously required subjects. (Id., Sect. 5.)

1899.— School Committee given full power over repairs and erection of new buildings. (Acts of 1899, Chap. 362.)

1899.— The attempt to abolish sub-committees having failed, they succeeded in obtaining an amendment to the rules restoring their power, and giving them a practical veto over all appointments, transfers and removals of teachers in their respective districts, thus partially overthrowing the reforms of the previous year. (S. M. of 1899, p. 300.)

First appropriation for playgrounds. (S. D. 3 of 1903, p. 122.)

Erection of Normal School building authorized (Acts of 1899, Chap. 239), but subsequently repealed. (Acts of 1901, Chap. 473, Sect. 8.)

Special classes for mentally deficient children established. (S. D. 4 of 1900, p. 51.)

1900.— Lectures on natural sciences, history and kindred subjects authorized. (Acts of 1900, Chap. 166.)

School teachers' retirement fund established. (Acts of 1900, Chap. 237; S. D. 19 of 1900, p. 8.)

Portable schoolhouses built to relieve temporary congestion of pupils in different sections of the city. (S. D. 19 of 1900, p. 26.)

Vacation Schools established for the first time under authority of Acts of 1899, Chap. 246. (S. D. 15 of 1900; S. D. 15 of 1902, p. 25.)

Elaborate report by Health Department (S. D. 6 of 1900) showing sanitary needs, and by Fire Department (S. D. 16 of 1900) showing fire protection needs for schools.

Quota of pupils to teachers reduced from 56 to 50 in grammar classes and two primary grades, and to 42 in the first primary grade. (S. D. 19 of 1900, p. 13; S. D. 3 of 1900, p. 7; S. D. 4 of 1900, p. 23; S. M. of 1900, p. 265.)

A corps of paid substitutes established to fill temporary vacancies in teaching force. (S. D. 19 of 1900, p. 14; S. D. 4 of 1900, p. 26.)

Reduction of grades in elementary schools from nine to eight recommended by Superintendent and Board of Supervisors (S. D. 3 of 1900, p. 19), and School Committee voted to instruct Board of Supervisors to prepare revised course providing for eight grades instead of nine. (S. M. of 1900, p. 244; S. D. 4 of 1900, p. 36.)

1901.— Schoolhouse Department established; loans of $1,000,000 annually for four years for new buildings, etc., authorized (Acts of 1901, Chap. 473), and School Committee given authority to appropriate annually from the tax rate 40 cents upon each $1,000 of taxable valuation for new schools. (Acts of 1901, Chap. 448.) Additional loan of $300,000 authorized to complete buildings then being erected. (Acts of 1901, Chap. 288.)

South Boston High School established (S. D. 3 of 1903, p. 52) and new high school buildings opened in Dorchester, East Boston and West Roxbury. (S. D. 15 of 1901, p. 18.)

1901.— Elective system for studies in high schools adopted. (S. D. 3 of 1901, p. 7 *et seq.*; S. D. 15 of 1901, p. 15.)

Experiment in school gardening conducted in connection with Normal School. (S. D. 11 of 1901, p. 5.)

Office of Schoolhouse Custodian established. (S. D. 15 of 1901, p. 16.)

Free evening lectures given under provisions of Acts of 1893, Chap. 208, and Acts of 1900, Chap. 166. (S. D. 15 of 1902, p. 32; S. D. 13 of 1903; S. D. 13 of 1904, p. 25.)

1902.— Petition to Legislature for authority to establish a Teachers' College in place of Normal School — Legislature gave leave to withdraw. (S. D. 3 of 1902, p. 12; S. D. 14 of 1903, p. 11.)

Unsuccessful attempt made to increase the course in the Normal School to three years. (S. M. of 1902, p. 507.)

Increased loans for new buildings authorized. (Acts of 1902, Chap. 386.)

Rules amended taking away power of sub-committees over appointments, transfers and removals of teachers, and requiring that the same be made by the Superintendent direct to the School Committee. (S. M. of 1902, p. 94.)

Appropriation from taxes for new buildings vetoed by Mayor. Later $90,000 appropriated for that purpose and approved by Mayor. (S. D. 15 of 1902, p. 50.)

The subject of the extended use of school buildings considered, and Educational Centres established (since merged in evening schools). (S. D. 15 of 1902, p. 17; S. D. 13 of 1904, p. 45; S. D. 7 of 1908, p. 54.)

Resolution adopted that sex should not be a bar to promotion in the teaching force, and that in any appointment to a position as principal of a girls' school, a woman, other things being equal, should be preferred. (S. D. 15 of 1902, p. 40; S. M. of 1902, p. 179.)

Power to license minors under 14 vested in Boston School Committee. (Acts of 1902, Chap. 531.) Rules provide that the minimum age for licensees shall be over 10. (S. M. of 1902, p. 462.)

A system of promotion of janitors for merit established. (S. D. 14 of 1903, p. 16.)

1903.— Appropriation of $60,000 authorized for maintenance of schools, out of "40 cents" fund. (Acts of 1903, Chap. 170.)

Valuable historical review of the Boston school system by Superintendent Seaver. (S. D. 3 of 1903.)

Report of the Committee on Extended Use of School Buildings, with an account of Educational Centres and Vacation Schools. (S. D. 9 of 1903.)

Uniform schedule of janitors' salaries adopted. (S. D. 11 of 1903; S. M. of 1903, p. 522.)

1904.— School Committee authorized to expend money for exhibition at any national, state or foreign exposition. (Acts of 1904, Chap. 172.)

1904.— Admission of men to Normal School authorized (Acts of 1904, Chap. 212) and entrance to the Normal School made more difficult, through examinations, in the hope of securing better teachers. (S. D. 9 of 1906, p. 12.)

The change from nine to eight grades below the high schools further considered. Superintendent Seaver said "the present opposition to a change is nothing more than a disinclination to change working habits. The waste of time that affects the course of very many of the abler pupils and the dawdling habits thereby engendered call for some effectual remedy." (S. D. 3 of 1904, pp. 48, 50, 73.)

Industrial education in elementary schools, introduced experimentally in Winthrop School. (S. D. 10 of 1910, p. 56.)

George H. Conley elected Superintendent. (S. M. of 1904, p. 302.)

Power of sub-committees over appointments, transfers and removals of teachers partially restored, the rules being amended to require that the same be first submitted to said committees, who are required, however, to report to the School Committee not later than one month thereafter. (S. M. of 1904, pp. 143, 173; S. D. 13 of 1904, p. 13.)

Elaborate report by Director of Drawing on the Evening Drawing Schools, their needs, possibilities of extension, and value in industrial training. (S. D. 3 of 1905.)

1905.— Compulsory school age raised to "under 16" where child cannot read and write English. (Acts of 1905, Chap. 320.)

Lincoln Day to be observed with appropriate exercises in the public schools. (Acts of 1905, Chap. 328.)

State released to city land on Newbury street, occupied by Horace Mann School, the proceeds, if sold, to be used for another site for the School for the Deaf. (Acts of 1905, Chap. 467.)

Further loan authorized for new buildings. (Acts of 1905, Chap. 392.)

Permission given to certain private charitable organizations to place trained nurses in certain schools without expense to the city, an experiment which led to the legislation as to nurses in 1907. (S. D. 17 of 1906, p. 51.)

Plans for Commercial High School adopted. (S. D. 4 of 1905; S. M. of 1905, p. 224.)

Walter S. Parker Acting Superintendent after Mr. Conley's death in December. (S. D. 9 of 1906, p. 8.)

School Committee reorganized and membership reduced to five (beginning January, 1906); elected at large. (Acts of 1905, Chap. 349.)

1906.— Board of Superintendents established (in place of Board of Supervisors), to consist of Superintendent and six assistant Superintendents, elected by School Committee for terms of one to six years, one assistant superintendent to be elected annually, after first election for six years. (Acts of 1906, Chap. 231.)

Stratton D. Brooks elected Superintendent for term of six years. (S. M. of 1906, p. 162.)

1906.— Rules and regulations revised, leaving details of administration to be performed by paid officials, with executive responsibility, while the duties of the School Board became mainly legislative. (S. D. 9 of 1906, p. 10.) The principle of direct accountability on the part of subordinates to superiors established. (S. D. 17 of 1906, p. 20.) System of sub-committees abolished. (S. D. 17 of 1906, p. 12.)

Office of Business Agent established and Auditor, Business Agent and Secretary elected on tenure. (Acts of 1906, Chap. 318.)

Board of Sale of school land and buildings established, consisting of the Mayor, School Committee and Schoolhouse Commission. (Acts of 1906, Chap. 259.)

Independent Industrial Schools authorized, the State to bear one-fifth, later increased to one-half the cost. (Acts of 1906, Chap. 505; Acts of 1909, Chap. 540.)

School athletics placed in charge of School Committee. (Acts of 1906, Chap. 251.)

Law amended so that physical or mental condition capable of correction no excuse, unless all reasonable measures are employed to correct the same, for a child's nonattendance at school. (Acts of 1906, Chap. 383.)

Appointment of School Physicians required by law, but not applicable to Boston where Board of Health maintains them. Every child in the public schools to be tested by teachers at least once a year for defective sight or hearing or other disability tending to prevent its receiving full benefit of school work. (Acts of 1906, Chap. 502.)

Ground for temporary exclusion of pupils from school extended to exposure to any infectious or contagious disease. (Acts of 1906, Chap. 371.)

Boston Juvenile Court established. (Acts of 1906, Chap. 489.)

Under the new Board the following measures for improving the school service undertaken or accomplished (see Superintendent's Report, S. D. 9 of 1906, and Annual School Report, S. D. 17 of 1906):

(1) Merit system of appointing teachers through a Civil Service system greatly strengthened.

(2) Change of requirements for teachers' certificates to secure teachers skilled in departmental work.

(3) System established of supervising and training teachers while serving as substitutes. Supervisor of Substitutes appointed.

(4) Promotional examinations or tests of efficiency required of teachers.

(5) A system established of leave of absence on half pay for purposes of study and travel to teachers who have served seven years, and leave of absence for rest after twenty years of service.

1906.— (6) Heads of departments established in high and Latin schools to secure uniformity of aim and greater effectiveness in teaching departmental subjects.
(7) Establishment of High School of Commerce.
(8) Revision of high school course of study, restricting somewhat the freedom of electives, and establishing certain required subjects. A full four years, or its equivalent, required to secure a diploma.
(9) Revision of Evening High School course of study to encourage pupils to pursue a regular course of serious work with final graduation in four years.
(10) Elimination of distinction between primary and grammar schools; both thereafter treated as elementary schools as distinguished from the high or secondary schools.
(11) Substitution of eight for nine grades in the elementary schools.
(12) Reorganization of manual training for girls, and appointment of a Supervisor of Household Science and Arts to have charge of cookery and sewing.
(13) Establishment of disciplinary classes for boys who might otherwise be sent to the Parental School.
(14) Election of a medical inspector for special classes.
(15) Uniting of drawing and manual training into one department, under one director.
(16) Evening and Vacation Schools united under one director.
(17) Evening class in salesmanship previously maintained at private expense taken into the school system.
(18) Appointment of Advisory Committee of Physicians to consider various health problems.

1907.— Power of School Committee in respect to physical education enlarged; special appropriations from tax rate (two cents for 1907 and four cents annually thereafter upon each $1,000 of taxable valuation) authorized for physical education and playgrounds, etc. (Acts of 1907, Chap. 295.)
School nurses authorized, with special appropriation from tax rate not exceeding $10,000 for 1907 and thereafter each year of 2 cents upon each $1,000 of taxable valuation. (Acts of 1907, Chap. 357.)
Physician's certificate to exempt child from vaccination must be "for cause stated therein." (Acts of 1907, Chap. 215.)
School Committee required each year to designate where additional school accommodations are necessary, and order in which they shall be provided; annual issue of bonds for new school buildings authorized. (Acts of 1907, Chap. 450.)
The following measures were begun or accomplished (see Superintendent's Report, S. D. 13 of 1907, and Annual School Report, S. D. 16 of 1907):
(1) Larger co-operation of the teaching force in determining educational policies.

1907.— (2) Readjustment of the high schools to the new system of eight grades in the elementary schools. A committee of conference known as the Committee on Betterment appointed for this purpose, consisting of the Superintendent and representatives of the Board of Superintendents, high and elementary school principals and teachers.

(3) Revision of course of study for elementary schools to meet the change in number of grades, prepared with the assistance of special committees consisting of one or more assistant Superintendents, Directors, principals and teachers.

(4) Reduction of quota of pupils in elementary schools to 48 in 1907, 46 in 1908, and thereafter 44.

(5) Reorganization of the Department of Physical Training as a Department of School Hygiene under a Director of Hygiene; school athletics placed under this department.

(6) System of training teachers strengthened by appointment of a Supervisor of Practice in the Normal School.

(7) High School of Practical Arts for Girls established.

(8) Industrial education extended in elementary schools through experiment in Hancock and Agassiz schools and continued in Winthrop School.

(9) Appointment of special advisory committees of laymen on various school subjects, notably the Committee for the High School of Commerce.

(10) Appointment of committee of teachers known as the Committee on College Credit to consider the opportunities for collegiate instruction open to teachers of Boston and vicinity.

(11) Extension of schedule of janitors' salaries to include high schools.

1908.— Pensions (maximum $180 per year) for members of the teaching or supervising staff required with special appropriations from tax rate of 5 cents annually on each $1,000 of taxable valuation. (Acts of 1908, Chap. 589.) Accepted by City Council June 22, 1908.

Instruction required by law to be given as to tuberculosis and its prevention. (Acts of 1908, Chap. 181.)

Provisions as to fire escapes. (Acts of 1908, Chap. 524.)

The following measures were begun or accomplished (see Superintendent's Report, S. D. 7 of 1908, and Annual School Report, S. D. 8 of 1908):

(1) Codification of teachers' certificate privileges, and list prepared of teachers arranged as to their eligibility for promotion.

(2) Teacher assigned to open-air class for tuberculous children on Parker Hill; later transferred to Refectory Building, Franklin Park.

(3) Teachers of sewing for the first time appointed on tenure, and the work reorganized under the Supervisor of Household Science and Arts.

(4) Departmental organization of the high schools completed by appointment of women as heads of departments with the rank of first assistants.

1908.— (5) Establishment of High School Councils, one for each department, consisting of the heads of departments of the various high schools, each school having one vote, to consider the important problems of courses of instruction, text-books, supplementary material and kindred subjects.

(6) Clerical assistants authorized in Latin and high schools to relieve principals from clerical work.

(7) Last year of the Vacation Schools, which this year in part and thereafter wholly were merged into the Summer Playgrounds.

(8) Committees of school principals established to advise Superintendent as to plans for new buildings.

(9) Exchange of teachers with Prussia arranged through the Carnegie foundation.

(10) Board of Apportionment established consisting of Board of Superintendents, Business Agent and Auditor.

(11) Rule established under which teachers retire at seventy years of age, and maximum age limit for new teachers placed at forty.

(12) Martin District organized as a model school for the pupils of the Normal School, with one of the Normal School teachers (Director of the Model School) as principal.

(13) One of the truant officers made Supervisor of Licensed Minors.

(14) Extension of term of evening schools for foreign-born pupils.

(15) Keeping of records in and making report by evening schools systematized.

(16) System of accounts adopted by the Business Agent to show the cost of each unit of the school system.

1909.— Appropriations allowed School Committee from the tax levy for general school purposes increased from $2.75 to $2.85 upon each $1,000 of taxable valuation in 1909–10, $2.95 in 1910–11, and $3.05 in 1911–12; each in addition to 25 cents for the repair fund, 40 cents for the new buildings fund, 4 cents for physical education, 2 cents for nurses, and 5 cents for pensions, upon each $1,000. (Acts of 1909, Chap. 388.)

School Committee given authority over secret (except religious) organizations of pupils. (Acts of 1909, Chap. 120.)

Display of United States flag on or in schools made compulsory. (Acts of 1909, Chap. 229.)

Loans authorized for High School of Commerce and administration building. (Acts of 1909, Chap. 446.)

Pensions for teachers — maximum pension $180. (Acts of 1909, Chap. 537.) Not accepted by School Committee, and repealed by Acts of 1910, Chap. 617.

The following measures were undertaken or completed (see Superintendent's Report, S. D. 13 of 1909, and Annual School Report, S. D. 15 of 1909):

1909.— (1) Trade School for Girls established, under provisions of Acts of 1906, Chap. 505, and Acts of 1909, Chap. 540, to be conducted by School Committee as agent of Board of Education, the State bearing part of the cost, the object of the school being to give a trade training to girls between fourteen and eighteen who are obliged to become wage earners.
(2) Summer High School opened in the Roxbury High School for those wishing to make up conditions, those preparing for college admission examinations and for admission to high schools.
(3) A committee on vocational advice appointed.
(4) Evening industrial schools take place of evening drawing schools, conducted by School Committee as agent of Board of Education, the State bearing part of the cost (under Acts of 1906, Chap. 505, and Acts of 1909, Chap. 540).
(5) Further experiments of an industrial character in the elementary schools introduced in the Eliot School, Washington Allston School, Lyman School, Oliver Wendell Holmes District, Quincy District and in the Horace Mann School.
(6) Pre-Apprentice School for Printing and Bookbinding established in East Boston.
(7) Experimental health or open-air rooms established.
(8) Manual for public school playgrounds issued and greater activity and system with respect to physical training. Provisional courses in physical education adopted both for the elementary and high schools. Weighing scales and measuring rods purchased to take records of each child's weight and height.
(9) Health Day observed in the schools and annual Health Day established.

1910.— New act passed providing annual pensions for members of the teaching and supervising staff retired under its provisions — minimum, after 30 years' service, $312; maximum, $600; also pensions of not less than $180 for not less than sixty annuitants of Teachers' Retirement Fund and other teachers described in the act. (Acts of 1910, Chap. 617.)
Instruction to be given in "thrift" authorized. (Acts of 1910, Chap. 524.)
Requirements as to military drill modified, exempting a pupil if his parent or guardian is of a religious denomination conscientiously opposed to bearing arms, or is conscientiously scrupulous of bearing arms; or upon certificate from a physician of good standing that it would be injurious to the pupil's health. (Acts of 1910, Chap. 201.)
The following measures have been established or considered:
(1) Teachers' council on pensions organized.
(2) Continuation schools established, wherein persons employed may receive part time instruction that will be of immediate assistance in their daily work. Title of Director of Evening and Vacation Schools changed to Director of Evening and Continuation Schools.

1910.— (3) New system of penmanship introduced.
- (4) Minimum age limit for admission to kindergartens raised to four years.
- (5) Clerical High School established by order passed February 7, 1910, to begin on July 11, 1910; order rescinded because of lack of funds June 6, 1910.
- (6) Newsboys' Trial Board established consisting of two adults appointed by School Committee and three licensed newsboys elected by their fellows.
- (7) Trial Board for Janitors established, consisting of the Secretary of the School Committee, the Business Agent, and a school janitor elected by his associates, to secure a careful investigation of complaints made against janitors, engineers or matrons.
- (8) Appropriation from annual taxes for new school buildings passed over Mayor's veto.

1911.— Savings banks authorized with consent of and under regulations approved by School Committee and Bank Commissioner to receive deposits from school children through the principal or teachers or by collectors. (Acts of 1911; Chap. 211.)

Penalty for failure to display United States flag on schoolhouses. (Acts of 1911, Chap. 232.)

School committees authorized to expend money for the supervision of sports and the equipment thereof. (Acts of 1911, Chap. 314.)

School committees authorized to grant use of school halls for public or educational purposes which will not interfere with regular school work. (Acts of 1911, Chap. 367.) Not yet accepted by the Boston City Council.

"Illiterate minor" defined by statute (for compulsory attendance at evening school) to mean an illiterate under the age of twenty-one years. (Acts of 1911, Chap. 241.)

Instruction authorized in the application of surgical remedies and first aid for the injured. (Acts of 1911, Chap. 247.)

School Committee authorized to appropriate an additional 10 cents in the year 1912, 20 cents in the year 1913, and thereafter annually 25 cents upon each $1000 of taxable valuation, to be used wholly for the purpose of increasing salaries of teachers. (Acts of 1911, Chap. 708.)

The following measures were begun or accomplished:
- (1) Establishment of the following new schools:
    - a. Boston Industrial School for Boys (taking over the Pre-Apprentice School for Printing and Bookbinding).
    - b. Evening Trade School.
    - c. Girls' Evening High School.
    - d. Continuation School class in household arts as a State-aided school.
- (2) Assumption by the School Committee of the financial control of all school athletics.

1911.— (3) Enlargement of the truant officers' force and the special assignment of one truant officer to the enforcement of the laws pertaining to evening school attendance.

(4) Adoption of a regulation requiring a small deposit for admission to evening high and industrial schools of persons not required by law to attend such schools, under Acts of 1911, Chap. 309.

(5) Appointment of a permanent force of playground teachers.

(6) Establishment of additional open-air classes in elementary schools.

(7) Removal of old and unauthorized text-books from the schools systematically begun.

(8) Adoption of a per capita plan of distribution of supplies and text-books in the schools.

INDEX.

	Page
Absence, leave of, for teachers	18, 24
Administration Building	27
Adults, schools for	9, 11, 13, 15, 28
Advisory committees	25, 26
African children, schools for	6
Agassiz School	26
Age limit for minors' licenses	22
Age limit for pupils	6, 7, 8, 9, 10, 11, 12, 13, 15, 18, 20, 23, 29
Age limit for teachers	27
Agriculture	12
Alcoholic drinks	16
Aldermen	7
Algebra	7, 11, 19
Annual reports by School Committee	9
Apparatus, free	16
Apportionment, Board of	27
Appropriations	6, 11, 12, 13, 17, 20, 22, 25, 26, 27, 29
Arithmetic	6, 9, 15
Astronomy	11
Athletics	24, 26, 29
Attendance at school	10, 13, 17, 18, 19, 20, 23, 24, 29
Auditing clerk	14
Auditor	24, 27
Behavior	6, 15
Betterment, committee on	26
Bible reading	11, 12, 14
Bishop, Nathan	10
Blackboards	8
Board of Apportionment	27
Board of Education, State	9, 12, 18, 28
Board of Health	18, 19, 21, 24
Board of Sale	24
Board of Superintendents	23, 26, 27
Board of Supervisors	14, 15, 16, 17, 19, 20, 21, 23
Bonds	19, 20, 21, 22, 23, 25, 27
Book-keeping	7
Books	7, 8, 11, 12, 13, 14, 16, 30
Boston Industrial School for Boys	29
Boston Juvenile Court	24
Botany	11
Brighton, annexation of	13
Brighton High School	9, 13

	Page
Brooks, Stratton D.	23
Buildings, school	13, 17, 18, 19, 20, 21, 22, 23, 24, 25, 27, 29
Business agent	24, 27
Calisthenics	15
Carpentry	15, 16
Certificates for teachers	5, 7, 12, 14, 24, 26
Chairs	11
Charlestown, annexation of	13
Charlestown High School	10, 13
Chemistry	11
Children's Institutions Department	19
Children, mentally deficient	21
Children's savings	29
Children, testing sight, hearing, etc.	24
City Council	9, 13, 17, 19, 20, 29
City medals for girls	7
Civil polity	11
Civil service	17, 18, 20, 24
Classes, size of	15, 17, 18, 21, 26
Clerical assistants	27
Clerical High School	29
Coeducation	8, 12, 18
College credit, committee on	26
Color, distinction on account of, forbidden	11
Colored children	6, 9, 11
Commerce, High School of	23, 25, 26, 27
Commercial courses	20
Committees, advisory	25, 26
Committee of Ten, report of	19
Common Council	8, 10
Common schools, beginning of	5
Compulsory school attendance	10, 13, 17, 18, 19, 20, 23, 24, 29
Conferences, teachers'	26
Conley, George H.	23
Conservatism, instance of	8
Constitutional amendment	11
Contagious diseases	16, 20, 24
Continuation schools	28, 29
Cookery	17, 19, 25
Corporal punishment	12
Councils, teachers'	25, 27, 28
Current expenses paid by loan	6
Custodian, Schoolhouse	22
Deaf, Horace Mann School for	13, 16, 18, 23, 28
Deare Island	5
Deer Island	17
Defective sight or hearing, testing of	24
Departmental instruction	19, 24, 25, 26
Departments, heads of	25, 26
Desks	11

	Page
Dictionaries	10
Diplomas	7, 13, 18, 25
Diphtheria	16
Disciplinary classes	25
Dorchester, annexation of	13
Dorchester High School	10, 13, 20, 21
Double-headed system	6, 8
Drawing	8, 9, 10, 13, 15, 20, 23, 25, 28
Drawing, director of, report	23
Drill, military	12, 15, 28
Dwight School, carpenter's class in	15
East Boston High School	14, 20, 21
Education, State Board of	9, 12, 18, 28
Educational Centres	22
Elective studies	22, 25
Elementary schools	5, 20, 23, 25, 26
Eliot, Charles W., President	19
Eliot High School	10
Eliot, Samuel	14
Eliot School	16, 28
Engineers	17, 29
English	5, 6, 9, 11, 20, 23
English Classical School	7
English High School	7, 8, 9
Evening drawing schools	13, 23, 28
Evening high schools	13, 17, 25, 29, 30
Evening industrial schools	13, 28
Evening schools	11, 12, 13, 15, 17, 18, 20, 22, 23, 25, 27, 28, 29, 30
Evening Trade School	29
Everett School	17
Examination papers of 1845	9
Examinations for diplomas	18
Examinations of teachers	7, 12, 14, 24
Exhibitions, appropriations for, authorized	22
Extended use of school buildings	22, 29
Fire protection needs	21, 26
First public school	5
Flags	19, 27, 29
Foreign-born pupils, evening schools for	27
Franklin medals	6
Franklin School	17
Free text-books	7, 10, 16
French	11, 19
Furniture	11, 18
Gardening	22
Geography	6, 9, 15
Geology	11
Geometry	7, 19
Girls, city medals for	7
Girls' Evening High School	29

Girls, first admitted to schools	6
Girls' High and Normal School	10, 13
Girls' High School	7, 8, 10, 11, 13
Girls' High School of Practical Arts	20, 26
Girls' Latin School	14
Girls, trade school for	28
Globes	8
Grades, beginning of system of nine	13
Grades, reduction from nine	19, 21, 23, 25, 26
Grammar	5, 6, 9, 20
Grammar masters	5, 6, 8, 9, 10, 12, 14, 15
Grammar schools	5, 6, 7, 8, 9, 10, 11, 13, 16, 17, 18, 19, 21, 25
Greek	6
Gymnastics	10, 15
Hancock School	16, 26
Hand tools	16, 18, 19
Harvard College	5, 7
Health Day	28
Health Department	18, 19, 21, 24
Hearing, defective, testing for	24
High schools	7, 8, 9, 12, 13, 15, 17, 20, 22, 23, 24, 25, 26, 27, 29, 30
High school councils	26
High schools, suburban, abolition proposed	15
Historical review of schools	22
History	7, 11, 15, 18, 21
Holidays	17
Horace Mann School	13, 16, 18, 23, 28
Household science and arts	25, 26, 29
Household science and arts, supervisor of	25, 26
Hyde School	17
Hygiene	10, 15, 16, 17, 18, 20, 26
Hygiene, director of	26
Hygiene, instructor in	15, 16, 18
Illiterate children	7
Illiterate minor	29
Independent industrial schools	24, 28, 29
Industrial education	13, 14, 15, 16, 18, 23, 24, 26, 28, 29, 30
Infant schools	8
Injured, first aid to, instruction in	29
Institute of Technology	7
Intellectual science	11
Intermediate schools	7, 9, 14
Janitors	13, 17, 22, 26, 29
Juvenile Court	24
Kindergartens	8, 13, 14, 17, 19, 29
Knitting	7
Latin	5, 6, 19
Latin schools	5, 14, 20, 24, 25, 26
Leave of absence for teachers	18, 24
Lectures	12, 18, 21, 22

	Page
Licensed minors	12, 14, 17, 22, 27
Lincoln Day	23
Loans	6, 19, 20, 21, 22, 23, 25, 27
Logic	7
Long Island	5
Lyman School	28
Mann, Horace	9
Manual training	16, 18, 20, 25
Maps	8
Martin District, model school	27
Matrons	29
Mayor	7, 8, 10, 16, 22, 24
Measles	20
Measuring rods	28
Mechanic Arts High School	14, 16, 17, 18
Medals	6, 7
Medical inspectors	14, 15, 18, 19, 24, 25
Medical inspector for special classes	25
Memorial Day	18
Mentally deficient children, classes for	21
Merit system	20, 22, 24
Military drill	12, 25, 28
Model school	27
Moral science	11
Music	8, 9, 11
Music, director of	11
National Educational Association	19
Natural philosophy	11
Natural sciences	18, 21
Nautical schools	14
Newsboys' trial board	29
Nonresident pupils	11
Nonsectarianism	7, 11, 12, 14
Normal School	10, 13, 15, 17, 18, 20, 21, 22, 23, 26
North End Industrial Home	16
Nurses	23, 25, 27
Oliver Wendell Holmes District	28
Open-air classes	26, 28, 30
Orthography	6, 15
Parallel courses of study	19
Parental School	17, 19, 25
Parker, Walter S	23
Pencils	8
Penmanship	29
Pensions	14, 26, 27, 28
Philbrick, John D	10, 11
Physical training	8, 10, 12, 17, 18, 25, 26, 28
Physical training, director of	18
Physicians, school	24
Physiology	10, 16, 20

	Page
Playgrounds	21, 25, 27, 28, 30
Political economy	11
Portable schoolhouses	21
Practical Arts, Girls' High School of	20, 26
Practice, supervisor of	26
Pre-Apprentice School	28, 29
Primary schools	7, 8, 9, 11, 12, 14, 15, 18, 21, 25
Primary school committee	7, 8, 9, 11
Promotional examinations	24
Promotions of teachers	24, 26
Prussia, exchange with	26
Pupils, number to a teacher	15, 17, 18, 21, 26
Qualifications, teachers' certificate of	5, 7, 12, 14, 24
Quincy School	10, 28
Quota of pupils to teachers	15, 17, 18, 21, 26
Race, distinction on account of, forbidden	11
Reading	5, 6, 9, 15
Recess, no, experiment	18
Reference books, free	16
Religion, distinction on account of, forbidden	11
Religious instruction	6, 7, 11, 12, 14
Reorganization of school system	6, 7, 8, 10, 11, 13, 14, 20, 23
Repairs, school	20
Retirement fund	21, 28
Retirement of teachers	27
Rhetoric	7
Roxbury, annexation of	13
Roxbury High School	10, 12, 13
Roxbury High School for Girls	11, 12
Salaries paid from loans	6
Salaries, special appropriation for	29
Sale, Board of	24
Salesmanship	25
Sanitary needs	21
Savings, children's	29
Scarlet fever	16
School buildings	13, 17, 18, 19, 20, 21, 22, 23, 24, 25, 27
School Committee	6, 7, 8, 9, 10, 12, 13, 14, 15, 17, 18, 19, 20, 21, 22, 23, 24, 27, 28, 29
School Committee incorporated	14
School Committee, Primary	7, 8, 9, 11
School halls, use of	29
Schoolhouse custodian	22
Schoolhouse Department	21, 24
School physicians	24
School system, reorganization of	6, 7, 8, 10, 11, 13, 14, 20, 23
Schools:	
continuation	28, 29
elementary	5, 20, 23, 25, 26
evening	11, 12, 13, 15, 17, 18, 20, 22, 23, 25, 27, 28, 29, 30

Schools: Page

    grammar.................5, 6, 7, 8, 9, 10, 11, 13, 16, 17, 18, 19, 21, 25

    high............7, 8, 9, 12, 13, 15, 17, 20, 22, 23, 24, 25, 26, 27, 29, 30

    household science and arts.............................. 25, 29

    industrial...24, 28, 29

    infant.. 8

    intermediate...7, 9, 14

    kindergarten............................8, 13, 14, 17, 19, 29

    Latin...................................5, 14, 20, 24, 25, 26

    Mechanic Arts...............................14, 16, 17, 18

    Normal...................10, 13, 15, 17, 18, 20, 21, 22, 23, 26

    Practical Arts.. 20, 26

    Pre-Apprentice... 28, 29

    primary......................7, 8, 9, 11, 12, 14, 15, 18, 21, 25

    summer... 28

    trade...14, 28, 29

    vacation..21, 22, 25, 26, 27

    writing...5, 6, 9, 15, 29

Schools, sectarian, appropriations for, forbidden................. 11

School supplies, free.. 16

Science... 11

Seating of pupils.. 18

Seaver, Edwin P...........................15, 16, 17, 19, 22, 23

Secondary education, report on................................. 19

Secretary... 14, 24

Secret organizations... 27

Sectarianism.......................................7, 11, 12, 14

Sectarian schools, appropriations for, forbidden................. 11

Selectmen... 5, 6, 7

Sewing...7, 9, 11, 14, 15, 25, 26

Sex, not a bar to promotion.................................... 22

Shaw, Chief Justice.. 8

Sight, defective, testing for.................................... 24

Singing... 9

Single desk and chair.. 11

Single-headed system... 8, 10

Slates... 8, 11

Smallpox... 16

South Boston High School....................................20, 21

Spectacle Island... 5

Spelling.. 6

Sports, supervision of... 29

State Board of Education.............................9, 12, 18, 28

Stationery... 11, 14

Street Commissioners.. 19

Sub-committees...................11, 14, 19, 20, 21, 22, 23, 24

Substitute teachers..16, 21, 24

Substitutes, Supervisor of..................................... 24

Suburban high schools, proposed abolition of................... 15

Summer High School.. 28

Sunday schools... 6

	Page
Superfluous employee	10
Superintendent	9, 10, 11, 14, 15, 16, 19, 20, 21, 22, 23, 26, 27
Superintendents:	
Nathan Bishop	10
John D. Philbrick	11
Samuel Eliot	14
Edwin P. Seaver	15
George H. Conley	23
Walter S. Parker (acting)	23
Stratton D. Brooks	23
Superintendents, Board of	23, 26, 27
Superintendent of licensed minors	14, 17, 27
Supervisors, Board of	14, 15, 16, 17, 19, 20, 21, 23
Supplementary reading	15
Supplies, per capita distribution of	30
Surveying	7
Tax limit for schools	20, 21, 22, 25, 26, 27, 29
Teachers	5, 7, 9, 10, 11, 12, 14, 16, 17, 18, 20, 21, 22, 23, 24, 25, 26, 27, 28, 29, 30
Teachers' certificates	5, 7, 12, 14, 24, 26
Teachers' college	22
Teachers, exchange with Prussia	27
Teachers' Mutual Benefit Association	17
Teachers' retirement fund	21, 28
Tennyson Street School	17
Tenure for teachers,	17, 26
Tenure for school officers	24
Text-books	7, 10, 11, 12, 13, 14, 16, 30
Thrift	28
Tools	16, 18, 19
Trade schools	14, 28, 29
Truant laws	10, 15, 19, 20
Truant officers	13, 14, 15, 17, 18, 30
Trust, power to hold property in	14
Tuberculosis	26
Ungraded classes	17
Unification of school system	8, 9, 10, 12, 15, 19, 20, 24
Unit costs	27
United States history	11
Vacations	17
Vacation schools	21, 22, 25, 27
Vaccination	11, 20, 25
Veto, Mayor's	16, 22, 29
Vivisection	19
Vocational advice	28
Voters, women	14
Ward representation	7, 8, 10
Washington Allston School	28
Weighing scales	28
Wells School	17

	Page
West Roxbury, annexation of	13
West Roxbury High School	10, 13, 20, 21
Winthrop School	16, 23, 26
Women, heads of departments	26
Women principals	22
Women voters	14
Writing	5, 6, 9, 15, 29
Writing masters	5, 6, 8, 10
Writing schools	5, 8, 9

CPSIA information can be obtained
at www.ICGtesting.com
Printed in the USA
BVHW04*1019190918
527934BV00014B/1061/P